Animal Peculiarity Volume 2 Part 3

By T.P Just

~~~

Copyright © 2012 by T.P Just. All rights reserved.

I0439298

Get All The Books In The Series:

Animal Peculiarity Volume 1 [1-8]
Animal Peculiarity Volume 2 [1-8]
<u>Just Enterprises</u>

Table of Contents

1. Prologue

THERE is perhaps nothing extraordinary in the fact that man is wise and just, takes great care to provide for his own children, -shows due consideration for his parents, seeks sustenance for himself, protects himself against plots, and possesses all the other gifts of nature which are his. For man has been endowed with speech, of all things the most precious, and has been granted reason, which is of the greatest help and use.

Moreover, he knows how to reverence and worship the gods. But that dumb animals should by nature possess some good quality and should have many of man's amazing excellences assigned to them along with man, is indeed a remarkable fact. And to know accurately the special characteristics of each, and how living creatures also have been a source of interest no less than man, demands a trained intelligence and much learning. Now I am well aware of the labour that others have expended on this subject, yet I have collected all the materials that I could; I have clothed them in untechnical language, and am persuaded that my achievement is a treasure far from negligible. So if anyone considers them profitable, let him make use of them; anyone who does not consider them so may give them to his father to keep and attend to.

For not all things give pleasure to all men, nor do all men consider all subjects worthy of study. Although I was born later than many accomplished writers of an earlier day, the accident of date ought not to mulct me of praise, if I too produce a learned work whose ampler research and whose choice of language make it deserving of serious attention.

2. The Camel of Bactria

I have heard that Camels live for fifty years, but I have ascertained that those from Bactria live as much as twice that number. The males which are used in battle, the Bactrians castrate, thereby ridding them of their violent and intemperate disposition while preserving their strength. But in the case of the females they cauterize those parts which inflame them to lust.

Seal in love with a Diver

Eudemus asserts that a Seal fell in love with a man whose habit was to dive for sponges, and that it would emerge from the sea and consort with him where there was a rocky cavern. Now this man was the ugliest of his fellows, but in the eyes of the Seal the handsomest. Perhaps there is nothing to wonder at, for even human beings have frequently loved the less beautiful of their kind, being quite unaffected by the best-looking and paying no attention to them.

The Water-snake, its bite

Aristotle says that when a man has been bitten by a Water-snake he at once exhales a most foul odour, so much so that nobody can come near him. He says also that forgetfulness descends upon the bitten man and a thick mist upon his eyes, and that madness ensues and a violent trembling, and that after three days he dies.

3. The Rock Dove

You must know that the Oenas (Rock-dove) is a bird and not, as some maintain a vine. And Aristotle says that it is larger than a ring-dove but smaller than a pigeon. In Sparta too, I hear, there are men called Oenadotherae (Rock- dove-catchers).

The Circe

The Circe may be said to differ from the falcon not only in sex but in its nature too.

The Blue-fowl

Blue-fowl' is its name; it is a bird; its ways are apart from man; it hates to linger in cities or to lodge in a house; it even avoids lingering in fields or where there are cottages and huts belonging to man; it likes desolate places and delights in mountain peaks and precipitous crags. It has no love even for the mainland or for pleasant islands, but for Scyros and any equally dreary, barren spot, generally destitute of human beings.

The Chaffinches

Chaffinches, it seems, are cleverer than man at predicting the future. For instance, they can tell when winter is coming, and they take the most careful precautions against an impending snowfall, and for fear of being overtaken they flee to the Wood- lands where the thick foliage affords them, as you might say, an asylum.

4. The Ruff

They say that the country about Parium and its neighbor Cyzicus are inhabited by birds black in appearance; from their shape you would say that they were hawks. But they do not touch flesh, are temperate in their appetite, and for them seeds are a sufficient meal.

And when late autumn sets in, a flock of these birds (they call them Memnons) resort to the land round Ilium, making straight for the tomb of Memnon. And the people who still inhabit the Troad assert that there is a tomb there dedicated to Memnon the son of Eos (Dawn); and since the actual dead body was borne through the air by his mother from the midst of the carnage to Susa (celebrated for this reason as 'Memnonian'), where it was awarded a becoming burial, the monument in the Troad is called after him to no purpose.

And so year by year the birds named after the aforesaid hero arrive and separate themselves into hostile factions and fight violently until half their numbers are killed, when the victors depart and return whence they came.

How this all comes to pass and for what reason, I have at the moment no leisure to speculate, nor yet to track down the mysteries of Nature. This however I will mention.

The aforesaid birds engage in this contest around the tomb of the son of Eos and Tithonus year after year, whereas the Greeks held but one contest in honour of Pelias, of Amarynceus, and even of Patroclus, and of Achilles the adversary of Memnon

5. Crete hostile to Owls

They say that the Owl is not found at all in Crete, and moreover that if it is introduced from abroad it dies. So it seems that Euripides un- critically represented Polyeidus as seeing this bird and thereby conjecturing that he would discover the dead son of Minos.

And I myself have ascertained that the Cretan histories, beside the facts already told, relate in verse and prose how Crete received from Zeus a boon-seeing that the island had nursed him and effected that famous concealment of him-, namely that it should be free of all noxious creatures born to do harm, that it should neither produce them nor support them if introduced from abroad.

And the island proves how potent this boon was, for it produces none of the aforesaid creatures. But if a man by way of trying and testing the extent of Zeus's favour imports one of these alien creatures, it has but to touch the soil and it dies.

6. And to Snakes

Accordingly snake-hunters from and to the neighboring Libya use devices of this kind. These charmers of venomous reptiles tame a great number and bring them for people to wonder at, and with them they import a load of soil from Libya sufficient for their need.

This they do by way of precaution, to prevent the snakes from meeting their death. With this object, when they arrive at the aforesaid island they do not put down their snakes until they have laid a bed of the imported soil. This done, they collect crowds and fill the unintelligent majority with amazement. Now as long as each snake remains coiled up and settled in its place, or rises up without however crossing the limit of its own native dust, so long it lives. If however it strays on to the alien soil which is strange and hostile to it, it dies, and naturally so.

For if the will of Zeus did not fail of effect in the case of Thetis, and would not fail in the case of any other person, far less, I think, will it prove ineffectual when his own nurse is concerned.

A monstrous Snake in the Indus

The river Indus is devoid of savage creatures; the only thing that is born in it is a worm, so they say, in appearance like those that are engendered in, and feed upon, timber. But these creatures attain to a length of as much as seven cubits, though one might find specimens both larger and smaller.
Their bulk is such that a ten-year-old boy could hardly encircle it with his arms. A single tooth is attached to the upper jaw, another to the lower, and both are square are and about eighteen inches long; and such is the strength of their teeth that they can crush with the greatest ease anything that they get between them, be it stone, be it animal, tame or wild. During the daytime they live at the bottom of the river, wallowing in the mud and slime; for that reason they are not to be seen. But at night they emerge on to the land, and whatever they encounter, whether horse or ox or ass, they crush and then drag down to their haunts and eat it in the river, devouring every member of the animal excepting its paunch.
If however they are assailed by hunger during the day as well, and should a camel or an ox be drinking on the bank, they slide furtively up and seizing firmly upon its lips, haul it along with the utmost force and drag it by sheer strength into the water, where they feast upon it. Each one is covered with a hide two fingers thick.

Its capture

The following means have been devised for hunting and capturing them. Men let down a stout, strong hook attached to an iron chain, and to this they fasten a rope of white flax weighing a talent, and they wrap wool round both chain and rope to prevent the worm biting through them.

On the hook they fix a lamb or a kid, and then let them sink in the river. As many as thirty men hold on to the rope and each of them has a javelin ready to hurl and a sword at his side. Wooden clubs are placed handy, should they need to deal blows, and these are of cornel-wood and very hard.

Then when the worm is secured on the hook and has swallowed the bait, the men haul, and having captured it and killed it, hang it up in the sun for thirty days. From the body there drips thick oil into earthenware vessels; and each worm yields up to ten cotylae.

The oil from its body

This oil they seal and bring to the Indian King; no one else is permitted to have so much as a drop. The rest of the carcase is of no use. Now the oil has this power: should you wish to burn a pile of wood and to scatter the embers, pour on a cotyle and you will set it alight without previously applying a spark. And if you want to burn a man or an animal, pour some oil over him and at once he is set on fire. With this, they say, the Indian King even takes cities that have risen against him; he does not wait for battering-rams or penthouses or any other siege-engines, for he burns them down and captures them.

He fills earthen vessels, each holding one cotyle,[half pint] with oil, seals them, and slings them from above against the gates. When the vessels touch the embrasures they are dashed into fragments; the oil oozes down; fire pours over the doors, and nothing can quench it.

And it burns weapons and fighting men, so tremendous are its force. It is how-ever allayed and put out if piles of rubbish are poured over it.

Such is the account given by Ctesias of Cnidus.

7. The Porpoise

The Porpoise is a creature like the dolphin, and it too has milk. Its colour is not black but resembles very deep blue. It breathes not through gills but through a blow-hole, for that is the name they give
to its air-passage. The Porpoise frequents Pontus and the sea round about and rarely strays beyond its familiar haunts.

The Victorious Hen

When a Hen has defeated a cock-bird in battle it gives itself airs from sheer delight and lets down Hen Wattles, not however to the same extent as cocks, although it does so and is filled with pride and struts more grandly.

A captured Dolphin

The Dolphin is believed to love its own kin, and here is the evidence. Aenus is a city in Thrace. Now it happened that a Dolphin was captured and wounded, not indeed fatally, but the captive was still able to live.

So when its blood flowed the dolphins which had not been caught saw this and came thronging into the harbor and leaping about and were plainly bent on some mischief.

At this the people of Aenus took fright and let their captive go, and the dolphins, escorting as it might be some kinsman, departed.

But a human being will hardly attend or give a thought to a relative, be it man or woman, in misfortune.

8. Monkey and Cats

In Egypt, says Eudemus, a Monkey was being pursued and Cats were the pursuers. S0 the Monkey fled as fast as he could and made straight for a tree. But the Cats also ran up very swiftly, for they cling to the bark and can also climb trees.
But as he was going to be caught, being one against many, he leapt from the trunk and with his paws seized the end of an overhanging branch high up and clung to it for a long While. And since the Cats could no longer get at him, they descended to go after other prey.
So the Monkey was saved by his own considerable exertions, and it was to himself, as was proper, that he owed the reward for his rescue.

Places hostile to certain animals

Aristotle says that the soil of Astypalaea is unfriendly to snakes; just as, according to the same writer, Rhenea is to martens. No crow can go up on to the Acropolis at Athens. Say that Elis is the mother of mules, and you say what is false.

The Cicadas of Locris and Rhegium

There is an agreement between the people of Rhegium and of Locris that they shall have access to, and shall cultivate, one another's lands. But the Cicadas of the two territories do not agree to this and are not of one and the same mind, for you will find the Locrian Cicada is completely silent in Rhegium, and the Cicada from Rhegium is absolutely voiceless among the Locrians.

What the cause of such an exchange may be neither I nor anyone else, save an idle boaster, can say. Only to Nature, you men of Rhegium and of Locris is it known.

At any rate there is a river separating the territories of Rhegium and Locris, and the banks are not so much as a hundred feet apart; for all that the Cicadas of neither side fly across it. And in Cephallenia there is a river which occasions both fertility and barrenness among Cicadas.

9. Bees and their King

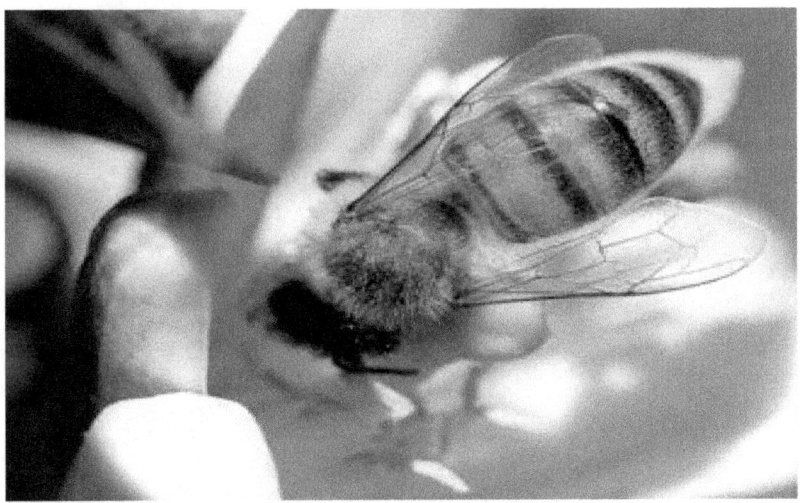

Bees when forsaken by their King, who is at once gentle and inoffensive and also stingless, give chase and pursue after the deserter from the post of rule. They track him down in some mysterious way and detect him by means of the smell he diffuses and bring him back to his kingdom of their own free will, indeed eagerly, for they admire his disposition.
But the Athenians drove out Pisistratus, and the Syracusans Dionysius, and other states their rulers, since they were tyrants and broke the laws and could not exhibit the art of kingship which consists in loving one's fellow-men and protecting one's subjects.

The King Bee and his state

It is the concern of the King Bee that his hive should be regulated in the following manner. To some bees he assigns the bringing of Water, to others the fashioning of honeycombs within the hive, while a third lot must go abroad to gather food.

But after a time they exchange duties in a precisely deter-
mined rotation. As to the King himself, it is enough for him to
take thought and to legislate for the matters that I mentioned
above after the manner of great rulers to whom philosophers
like to ascribe simultaneously the qualities of a citizen and of a
king.

For the rest he lives at ease and abstains from physical labour.
If however it is expedient for the bees to change their
dwelling, then the ruler departs, and if he happens to be still
young, he leads the way and the rest follow; if however he is
elderly, he is carried on his way and conveyed by other bees.
At signal bees retire to slumber. When it seems to be time to
go to sleep the King commands one bee to give the signal for
going to rest. And the bee obeys and gives the word,
whereupon the bees that have been buzzing till then retire to
bed.

Now so long as the King survives, the swarm flourishes and
all disorder is suppressed. The drones gladly remain at rest in
their cells, the older bees dwell in their quarters apart, the
young in theirs, the King by himself, and the larvae in their
own place.

Their food and their excrement are in separate places. But
when the King dies, disorder and anarchy fill the place; the
drones produce offspring in the cells of the bees; the general
confusion no longer permits the swarm to thrive, and finally
the bees perish for want of a ruler.

The Bee, its temperate life

The Bee leads a blameless life and would never touch animal food. It has no need of Pythagoras for counselor, but flowers afford it food enough. It is in the highest degree temperate; at any rate it abhors luxury and delicate living; witness the fact that it pursues and drives away a man who has perfumed himself, as if he were some enemy who has perpetrated actions past all remedy. It recognises too a man who comes from an unchaste bed and him also it pursues, as though he were its bitterest foe.

Its courage

And Bees are well-endowed with courage and are undaunted. For instance, there is not a single animal from which they flee; they are not mastered by cowardice but go to the attack. Towards those who do not trouble them or start to injure them or who do not approach the hive bent on mischief and with evil intent they show themselves peaceful and friendly; but against those who would injure them the fires of a truceless war, as the phrase goes, are kindled; and anyone who comes to plunder their honey is reckoned among their enemies. And they sting even wasps severely.

Its Sting

And Aristotle records its stills how Bees once finding a horseman near the hive attacked him violently and slew both, him and his horse. And further, they fight with one another and the stronger party defeats the weaker.

Its enemies

But I learn that toads and frogs from pools, bee-eaters, and swallows defeat them, and frequently wasps do so too. Yet the victor achieves what you might call a Cadmean victory, for he comes off badly from their blows and stings, since the Bees are armed with courage no less than with stings.

But Bees are not without a share of the wisdom of foresight, and Aristotle vouches for my statement thus. Some Bees came to a hive that was not theirs but a different one and proceeded to plunder the honey which did not belong to them.

But the Bees which were being despoiled of their labours nevertheless remained quiet and waited patiently to see what would happen. Then, when the bee- keeper had killed the greater number of the enemy, the Bees in the hive realised that they were in fact sufficient to sustain an equal combat and emerged to strike back, and the penalty which they exacted for the robbery left nothing to cavil at.

The Bee, its industry

Here is further evidence of the industry of Bees. In the coldest countries from the time when the Pleiads have set until the vernal equinox they continue at home and stay quiet in the hive, longing for the warmth and shunning the cold.

But for the rest of the year they abhor indolence and repose and are good at hard labour. And you would never see a Bee idling unless it was during the season when their limbs are numb with cold.

The Bee, its skill

Bees practice geometry and produce their graceful figures and beautiful conformations without any theory or rules of art, without what the learned call a 'compass.'

Its colonies

And when their numbers increase and the swarm thrives they send out colonies just as the largest and most populous cities do.

As Weather-prophet

Now the Bee knows when there is rain that threatens to persist, and when there will be a gale. But if surprised

By a wind, you will see every Bee carrying a pebble between the tips of its feet by way of ballast.

Its love of song

What the divine Plato says of cicadas and their love of song and music one might equally say of the choir of Bees. 'For instance, when they frolic and roam abroad, then the bee-keepers make a clashing sound, melodious and rhythmical, and the Bees are attracted as by a Siren and come back again to their own haunts.

Rats in Gyarus and Teredon

In the island of Gyarus Aristotle says that there are Rats and that they actually eat iron ore. And Amyntas says that the Rats of Teredon (this is in Babylonia) adopt the same food.

Scorpions on mt Latmus

I am told that on Latmus in Caria there are Scorpions which inflict a fatal sting on their fellow-countrymen; strangers however they sting lightly and just enough to produce an itching sensation. This in my opinion is a boon bestowed upon visitors by Zeus, Protector of the Stranger.

10. The King Wasp

Wasps also are subject to a King, but not, as men are, to a despot. Witness the fact that their Kings also are stingless. And their subjects have a law that they shall construct their combs for them. But although the rulers are twice the size of a subject, yet they are gentle and of a nature incapable of doing an injury either willingly or unwillingly.

Who then would not detest the Dionysii of Sicily, Clearchus of Heraclea, Apollodorus the oppressor of Cassandrea, Nabis the scourge of Sparta, if they trusted in the sword, when the King Wasps trust to their lack of sting and to their gentle nature?

The Wasp and its poison

This is what Wasps that are armed with a sting are said to do. When they observe a dead viper they swoop upon it and draw poison into their sting. It is from this source, I fancy, that men have acquired that knowledge and no good knowledge either. 'Seeking a deadly drug, that he might have wherewithal to smear his bronze-tipped arrows.'

Or again, to be sure (if one can trust the story),just as Heracles dipped his arrows in the venom of the Hydra, so do Wasps dip and sharpen their sting.

The Fly

Let not the Fly lack the honour of a mention in this record of mine, for it too is Natures handiwork
The Flies of Pisa at the season of the Olympic festival make peace, so to speak, both with visitors and with the local inhabitants.

11. The Great Sea Perch

The Great Sea Perch is a marine creature, and if you were to catch and cut it up, you would not then and there see it dead, but it retains the power of movement, and for a considerable time. All through the winter it likes to remain at home in its caverns, and its favourite resorts are near the land.

The Hake

The Hake has its heart in its belly, as experts in these matters agree and inform us.

12. The Peacock

The Peacock knows that it is the most beautiful of birds; it knows too wherein its beauty resides; it prides itself on this and is haughty, and gathers confidence from the plumes which are its ornament and which inspire strangers with terror.

In summertime they afford it a covering of its own, unsought, 'not adventitious. If, for instance, it wants to scare somebody it raises its tail-feathers and shakes them and emits a scream and the bystanders are terrified, as though scared by the clang of a hoplite's armour.

And it raises its head and nods most pompously, as though it were shaking a triple plume at one. When however it needs to co0l.itself it raises its feathers, inclines them in a forward direction and displays a natural shade from its own body, and wards off the fierceness of the sun's rays.

But if there is a wind behind it, it gradually expands its feathers, and the breeze which streams through them, blowing gently and agreeably, enables the bird to cool itself. It knows when it has been praised, and as some handsome boy or lovely woman displays that feature which excels the rest, so does the Peacock raise its feathers in orderly succession; and it resembles a flowery meadow or a picture made beautiful by the many hues of the paint, and painters must be pre- pared to sweat in order to represent its special characteristics.

And it proves how ungrudgingly it exhibits itself by permitting bystanders to take their fill of gazing, as it turns itself about and industriously shows all the diversity of its plumage, displaying with the utmost pride an array surpassing the garments of the Medes and the embroideries of the Persians.

It is said to have been brought to Greece from foreign lands. And since for a long while it was a rarity, it used to be exhibited to men of taste for a fee, and at Athens the owners used on the first day of each month to admit men and women to study them, and they made a profit by the spectacle.

They used to value the cock and the hen at ten thousand drachmas, as Antiphon says in his speech against Erasistratus.

For their maintenance a double establishment and custodians and keepers are needed. Hortensius the Roman was judged to have been the first man to slaughter a Peacock for a banquet. But Alexander of Macedon was struck with amazement at the sight of these birds in India, and in his admiration of their beauty threatened the severest penalties for any man who slew one.

Mouse saved from drowning

When Mice fall into cooling-vessels, since they cannot get out by swimming, they fasten their teeth into one another's tails, and then the first pulls the second and the second the third. In this way has Nature in her supreme wisdom taught them to combine and help one another.

The Crocodile

This is the way in which Crocodiles lie in wait for those who draw water from the Nile: they cover themselves with driftwood and, spying through it, swim up beneath it. And the people come bringing earthen vessels or pitchers or jugs. Then, as men draw water, the creatures emerge from the driftwood, leap against the bank, and seizing them with overpowering force make a meal of them. So much for the innate wickedness and villainy of Crocodiles.

13. The Bustard and Hounds

The Hare dreads Hounds, and so too does the rouse a boar
from the brake, and will bring a lion to bay, and pursue a stag.
Yet there is not a single bird that cares anything for a Hound,
but there is peace between them.

The Bustard alone is afraid of Hounds, the reason being that
these birds are heavy and carry a burden of flesh about with
them. Their wings do not easily lift them and carry them
through the air, so they fly low along the ground, weighed
down by their bulk. Hence they are frequently captured by
Hounds.

And since they, are aware of this, whenever they hear the bark
of Hounds, they run away into thickets and swamps, using
these as a protection and escaping instant danger without
difficulty.

The Lamb

The human child is slow to recognise its parents: it is taught and, one might say, compelled to look at its father, to greet its mother, and to smile upon its relatives. Whereas Lambs from the day of their birth gambol about their dams and know what is strange and what is akin to them. They have no need to learn anything from their shepherds.

The Monkey

The Monkey is a most imitative creature, and any bodily action that you teach it it acquires exactly, so as to be able to display its accomplishment. For instance, it will dance, once it has learnt, and if you teach it, will play the pipe. And I myself have even seen it holding the reins, laying on the whip, and driving a chariot. And once it has learnt whatever it may be, it would never disappoint its teacher. So versatile and so adaptable a thing is Nature.

Peculiarities of Certain Animals

Here are further examples of the peculiar and diverse natures of animals. Theopompus reports that in the country of the Bisaltae the Hares have a double liver. According to Ister the Guinea-fowls of Leros are never injured by any bird of prey. Aristotle says that among the Neuri the Oxen have their horns on their shoulders and Agatharcides says that in Ethiopia the Swine have horns. Sostratus asserts that all Blackbirds on Cyllene are White. Alexander of Myndus says that in Pontus the Flocks grow fat upon the bitterest Wormwood.
He states also that Goats born on Mimas do not drink for six months; all they do is to look towards the sea with their mouths open and to drink in the breezes from that quarter. I learn that the Goats of Illyria have a solid, not a cloven hoof. And Theophrastus has the most amazing statement that in Babylonia the fish frequently come out of the river and pasture on dry land.

14. The Purple Coot

Now the Purple Coot, in addition to being extremely jealous, has, I believe, this peculiarity: they say that it is devoted to its own kin and loves the company of its mates. At any rate I have heard that a Purple Coot and a Cock were reared in the same house that they fed together, that they walked step for step, and that they dusted in the same spot.

From these causes there sprang up a remarkable friendship between them. And one day on the occasion of a festival their master sacrificed the Cock and made a feast with his household. But the Purple Coot deprived of its companion and unable to endure the loneliness, starved itself to death.

Geese in love with human beings

In Aegium, a city of Achaia, a good-looking boy, an Olenian by birth, of the name of Amphilochus, was loved by a Goose. The boy was kept under guard with exiles from Olenus in Aegium, and so the Goose used to bring him presents.

In Chios Glauce, the harp-player, being a woman of extraordinary beauty, was adored by men, not that there is anything wonderful in that, but I am told that a Ram and a Goose also fell in love with her.

Geese and Eagles

When Geese cross the Taurus range they go in fear of the eagles; so each of them bites on a pebble to prevent it from uttering its cry, just as though they had gagged themselves, and so they cross in silence and by these means generally slip past the eagles.

Habits and food

The Goose being of a very hot and fiery nature is fond of bathing and delights in swimming, and prefers very moist fare, grass, lettuce, and all other things that generate coolness in its body. But even if it is exhausted with hunger it will not eat a bay-leaf or touch a rose-laurel either willingly or against its will, for it knows that if it eats either of them it will die.

Human victims of food and drink

Yet men through their unbridled appetites are the victims of plots against their food and drink. At any rate countless numbers have swallowed some bane while drinking, like Alexander or in food, like Claudius the Roman and Britannicus, his son.
And having fallen asleep from a dose of poison, they never rose again, some having drunk it deliberately, others because they were the victims of a plot.

The Egyptian Goose

The Egyptian Goose owes its composite name (goose-fox) to the innate peculiarities of the two creatures. It has the appearance of a goose, but for its mischievousness it might most justly be compared to the fox.

It is smaller than a goose but more courageous, and is a fierce fighter. For instance, it defends itself against an eagle, a cat, and all other animals that come against it.

Anatomy of the Snake

The following features are peculiar to the Snake. The heart has its allotted place close to the throat, the gall in the intestines; its testicles are close to the tail; the eggs which it produces are long and soft; its poison is contained in the fangs.

The Peacock

The Peacock (I have described the bird above) has these further innate peculiarities which are worth knowing. When three years old it begins to be pregnant and lays its eggs, and then starts to assume that many-coloured and beautiful plumage. But it does not brood upon its eggs immediately, but passes over two days. And the Peacock, like other birds, may from time to time lay a wind-egg.

Get All The Books In The Series: